Ghost Night

A play

John Grange and Peter Vincent

Samuel French—London
New York-Toronto-Hollywood

Copyright © 2004 by Peter Vincent
All Rights Reserved

GHOST NIGHT is fully protected under the copyright laws of the British Commonwealth, including Canada, the United States of America, and all other countries of the Copyright Union. All rights, including professional and amateur stage productions, recitation, lecturing, public reading, motion picture, radio broadcasting, television and the rights of translation into foreign languages are strictly reserved.

ISBN 978-0-573-02366-8

www.samuelfrench.co.uk

www.samuelfrench.com

FOR AMATEUR PRODUCTION ENQUIRIES

UNITED KINGDOM AND WORLD EXCLUDING NORTH AMERICA

plays@SamuelFrench-London.co.uk

020 7255 4302/01

Each title is subject to availability from Samuel French, depending upon country of performance.

CAUTION: Professional and amateur producers are hereby warned that GHOST NIGHT is subject to a licensing fee. Publication of this play does not imply availability for performance. Both amateurs and professionals considering a production are strongly advised to apply to the appropriate agent before starting rehearsals, advertising, or booking a theatre. A licensing fee must be paid whether the title is presented for charity or gain and whether or not admission is charged.

The professional rights in this play are controlled by Berlin Associates, 7 Tyers Gate, London SE1 3HX.

No one shall make any changes in this title for the purpose of production. No part of this book may be reproduced, stored in a retrieval system, or transmitted in any form, by any means, now known or yet to be invented, including mechanical, electronic, photocopying, recording, videotaping, or otherwise, without the prior written permission of the publisher. No one shall upload this title, or part of this title, to any social media websites.

The right of Peter Vincent to be identified as author of this work has been asserted in accordance with Section 77 of the Copyright, Designs and Patents Act 1988.

CHARACTERS

Madge, neat and efficient; 40s
Bella, worldly and attractive; 45
Consuela, elegant and well-spoken; 45
Nadia, dressed by Oxfam; 30
Charley, a "New Age" woman in jeans and a sweater; 35
Vera, dresses to please herself; 60+
Wendy, a very nervous type in a tracksuit; 25
Malcolm, a personable young man; 25

The action of the play takes place in a room in a haunted house

Time — the present

GHOST NIGHT

A room. Evening

The room has two entrances, one of which is covered by a curtain. The furnishings have certain additions, some of which have a somewhat disturbing effect. There is a small table covered with a cloth that descends to the floor and with an old-fashioned lamp, a Bakelite dial telephone (circa 1950) and a large china jug standing on it. There is a chair covered with an old, none-too-clean sheet with two cushions beneath it. Also in the room are a tribal mask, a stuffed animal, an old television with its screen turned away from the audience, an old-fashioned mains radio and a wind-up gramophone with a pile of 78 rpm records nearby

When the CURTAIN *rises the stage is in darkness apart from a dim glow in the hallway beyond the uncurtained door. A 78 rpm dance record is playing on the gramophone*

After a few seconds the record runs down

The door opens. Madge and Bella enter; Madge has a torch and a bag

Madge Hallo? Anyone there?
Bella (*half scared, half giggly*) Switch the light on, Madge. This place is giving me the creeps already.
Madge It's supposed to, Bella. It's a haunted house. (*She switches the lights on*)
Bella There's nobody here. Lucky you found the key under that plastic frog. We'd have been still out there in the rain.

Madge They said the house would be opened up for us.
Bella (*looking around the room*) No-one lives here, surely!
Madge But we heard music, didn't we?
Bella Oh, yes ... (*She confronts the tribal mask*) Eurgh! Where'd they get him?
Madge Do people *still* put dust sheets on chairs when they go away?
Bella There must be someone here, Madge. Someone or something wound up that gramophone!
Madge (*calling out*) Hallo? Anyone there? We're here!
Bella (*calling*) Dr Vulpus? (*To Madge*) Are you sure you got the right day?
Madge 'Course. (*She produces a programme of events and glances at it*) "Tuesday. Eight o'clock. Trip to Local Haunted House with celebrated psychic, Dr Igor Vulpus."
Bella Madge! Let's leave before something nasty happens ...
Madge That's typical of you! Why should something nasty happen?
Bella 'Cos I haven't got my dreamcatcher with me. Something always happens when I haven't got it.
Madge It's ghosts, dear, not Navajo Indians. Now keep calm. The others'll be arriving soon.
Bella (*looking at the chair covered by a sheet*) Well, I'm not looking under there for a start.
Madge Could be a body. Previous owner. Died of fright.
Bella Oh, don't! I'm jumpy as it is! Come on — let's go!
Madge Bell, you're letting your imagination run away with you!
Bella Well, it's too quiet — and there's a sort of whispering ... (*Picking up one of the records and reading the label*) "The Headless Horseman". (*She drops the record*)
Madge Gawd, Bella! What made you do that?
Bella I don't know. It was like something plucked it out of my hand!
Madge No, it didn't. Fit it back together. Shove it in the pile. No one'll know.
Bella (*putting the record back in the pile*) I remember when I spilt hot tea on my auntie's settee. I sat on it for two hours to dry it out.
Madge Shh! Someone coming.
Bella Oh, bloody hell! Let's hide!

Madge It's not a ghost. It's clumping. Oh, it's Consuela.

Consuela enters carrying an umbrella

Consuela I've had to park halfway up the road. I thought if this is a famous haunted house I expect a car park at least. You get a tea shop at Borley Rectory. Where's this famous Dr Vulpus?
Madge Well, he said he'd be here but the whole house seems deserted.
Bella (*pointing to the chair with the sheet*) Perhaps he's under there.
Consuela Why? Is he a druid or something? Or just terribly shy? (*She pokes the chair with her umbrella*) Nothing there. Well, I don't believe in ghosts anyway.
Madge You wanted to come, love.

A flickering light comes up from the television

Consuela I wanted to get out of the house. My husband's chiropractor comes round. I don't know what she does to his back but it's not getting any better. And he still keeps booking her at fifty pounds a session.
Madge (*sotto voce*) There goes his disability pension.

Bella wanders round to look at the television screen

Bella Here! This is on!
Consuela Well, what of it? As long as it's not showing the football. Or darts. Who wants to see some fatty throwing feathers at a bit of cork?
Bella It wasn't on when we came in.

There is a pause

Madge It must have been. These things don't switch themselves on. Unless ...
Bella Oh ... I feel someone's just walked right through me!
Consuela Oh, Bella, really. It's probably indigestion.

The television flicker fades

Madge It's gone off. That's strange.
Bella I think strange things are waiting to happen to all of us. My last husband was an embalmer, you know.
Consuela Is that why you used to look so well?
Bella I'll ignore that as always. Anyway, Mortimer, that's my last husband, was working late one night glazing this corpse up the undertakers' — 'cos he never brought work home. I put a block on that. Anyway, this corpse, suddenly its eyes open like that (*she demonstrates*) and its ears start to twitch. My Mort's hair went white overnight. Even under his armpits.
Consuela Do we have to have anatomical details? I've had a large tea and ——
Bella It turned out to be a short circuit in the work bench. Lucky for that man he was dead. 'Cos it would have killed him.
Consuela Oh, Bella, really, you should know (*better*) …
Madge (*interrupting*) Shhh! What's that?
Consuela What's what? I didn't hear anything.

They listen

Madge Could be the people next door. (*She relaxes. During the following she opens her bag and takes out a thermos and packets of biscuits*)
Bella Next door's a cemetery.
Nadia (*off*) Is it upstairs?
Charley (*off*) No, no. It's this way. There's a light …
Consuela Oh, it's Charley and Nadia. (*Calling*) Come in, you two ghosts and terrify these silly women.

Charley and Nadia enter

Charley Oh, thank God they're here!
Consuela Why were you two creeping?
Nadia When you're in the presence of the other side — you travel warily.

Ghost Night

Consuela Oh, for heaven's sake!
Charley This is all rather quaint! In another five years these will be antiques!
Nadia I feel there's a presence here ...
Charley (*making New Age gestures*) Oh yes! It needs atmosphere. I've got some joss sticks. How about sandalwood?
Consuela We've come for a lecture. Not a fumigation session.
Nadia I wonder how many people have passed away in this room?
Consuela You always say things like that! You said there was a ghost in Tesco's. At the fish counter.
Nadia There was. He looked like Charles the First.
Consuela Not in Tesco's surely. Waitrose, possibly ...
Charley Where did they get this furniture from? Ten Rillington Place?
Bella Oh, don't!
Charley They clearly don't know about Feng Shui.
Bella Can't stand Chinese food.
Charley That table's totally blocking the energy.
Nadia I'm sure I'm going to meet Arthur tonight.
Bella It's ghosts, Nadia, not a séance.
Nadia If you feel a sudden cold draught, that's Arthur.
Consuela Doing what, dear?
Nadia Wagging his tail of course.
Madge (*aside to Consuela*) She is having counselling.
Nadia Counselling? Who is?
Charley (*indicating the sheet on the chair*) What's underneath there?
Consuela Why don't you look?
Charley Didn't *you* look?
Bella We didn't like to. It's like — looking under a Scotsman's kilt. You never know what you'll find.
Charley Well, where's this Dr Vulpus then? He's supposed to start at eight.
Madge The agency said he was dead reliable.
Charley Can't we ring his mobile?
Madge He doesn't believe in mobiles. He's clairvoyant.
Bella Then he must have known he was going to be late.

Nadia Then why hasn't he called us?
Madge He doesn't know the number. When I booked him he suggested we bring a dog along. For the poltergeists.
Bella We haven't got a dog.

Nadia starts to sob

Madge Oh, Nadia! That dog of yours was very old. In dog terms he was a hundred and eighty-six.

The phone rings. Everyone looks at it

Madge Is anyone going to answer that?
Bella We can't do that. It's private.
Madge It might be Vulpus.

Bella picks up the receiver

Bella (*into the phone*) Hallo? ... Three-three-four-o it says here ...? Hallo? (*To the others*) They've rung off.
Consuela Try one-four-seven-one.
Bella The numbers are all rubbed out.
Madge I hate it when they ring off like that.
Nadia I'm picking up some nasty vibrations. I should never have come. I should never have come! I've got this weak heart as it is. Anything scary could ... Well ...
Consuela Your partner should never have let you come!
Nadia He said it would do me good. It was the same with the bungee jump.
Bella Are you sure he's the right person for you, Nadia?
Madge Shh!
Consuela Madge! Will you stop shushing!
Madge There's a humming sound.
Consuela What? Like bees?
Charley No ... I know that sound. It's a washing machine.
Bella There's — someone in the kitchen.
Nadia Oh! That'll be Dr Vulpus. He's been there all the time!

Consuela Why should he be hiding away in the kitchen?
Nadia Feeling the walls probably. That's what most ghost hunters do.
Bella My doctor always feels my chest. No matter what I've got wrong. He says it's holistic.
Consuela Madge, you go in the kitchen and see what it is.
Madge All right. Hang on! Why me? I'm not going on my own.
Consuela Well, if you're frightened I'll come with you.
Charley Me too. Safety in numbers.
Nadia But that will leave only two of us in here.
Consuela Oh, don't be silly. We're all grown-ups, aren't we? Well, aren't we? Oh, come on.

Consuela exits with Madge and Charley

Bella Talking of kitchens — that reminds me! You know I think I left the gas on when I come out.
Nadia Last week you said you left the bath running.
Bella I did. When I got home there was a waterfall down the stairs. But just before I came tonight, I'm sure I put a kettle on the gas and I don't remember taking it off. There could be a fire.
Nadia When it boils over it puts the flame out.
Bella Oh, bloody hell! Then the house'll be full of gas. It could blow up or take off. I'll have to pop home and check, eh?
Nadia No, Bella, don't go! It's better if we all stay together.
Bella If you're worried, come with me. We'll leave a note for the others.
Nadia I can't go home. I'll only have to read *The Adventures of Tintin* to Tabby for the hundredth time.
Bella If you read slowly little Tabby will fall asleep.
Nadia Tabby's my great aunt. She's eighty-eight.
Bella You're right. You're better off staying here.

There is a tapping noise from the hall

Nadia That could be Dr Wotsit!
Bella (*calling; nervously*) Dr Vulpus? In here!

Vera enters. She walks with a stick

Vera Oh dear, those bloody steps. I told Madge I can't go anywhere there's steps. And it's perishing in here! I think it's warmer outside than in here.
Nadia Oh, you've noticed it too. Keep your coat on. I have.
Bella They certainly didn't put no heating on for us. This wall's cold as ice.

Consuela and Madge enter

Consuela They left the washing machine on, that was all.
Madge And the tea towels are still damp. (*She sees Vera*) Oh, Vera. You're here! How's the legs?
Vera I'm cold. It's colder here than it is over there.
Consuela That's the central heating.
Madge I don't think there is any.
Consuela Shhh!
Madge Who's shushing now?
Consuela No! Shhh!

Wendy enters carrying a suitcase

Wendy Oh. Thank goodness. It's so dark out there! And I dragged this for miles.
Madge Why? What for, Wendy? Why bring a suitcase to a lecture?
Wendy I can. Why not? (*She puts the case down*)
Consuela (*moving the suitcase*) Heavens! What have you got in here? The Elgin Marbles?
Vera Consuela, she doesn't have to tell anyone what she's got in her suitcase ... So what *have* you got in there then?
Wendy Oh, all right. I've left Malcolm.
Nadia Where?
Wendy No. I've left him.
All (*except Wendy*) Why?

Pause

Nadia She doesn't want to say.
Wendy I shouldn't have come but tonight I was all alone in the flat and I'm frightened of being alone.
Consuela (*aside*) She's frightened of everything.
Vera Why didn't you get a taxi, love?
Wendy Oh, no thank you. You sit alone in the back of those things. They could take you anywhere. It's the same with lifts.
Madge Get a car, Wendy.
Wendy Oh, I couldn't drive. All alone in all that traffic. What if you broke down? And there could be a man hiding in the boot.
Bella All right if he's from the AA.
Wendy But I'm not a member.
Madge Well, you're not alone now, love. There's seven of us here.
Nadia No. Six.
Madge There's someone missing — who's missing?
Charley (*off; making a ghostly sound*) Wooooooooooo!

Everyone jumps. Wendy shrieks

Consuela (*surprisingly edgy*) Who's that being stupid? Scaring everybody!

Charley enters from behind the curtain

Charley It was just a joke ...
Consuela How did you get here like that?
Charley There's a passage from the kitchen. These are old houses. They've got bits left over from Edwardian days ... Come and see.
Consuela We'll take your word for it.
Charley I stumbled over something in the dark. A sack of potatoes or — something.
Vera Or something.
Madge Oughtn't we better look? I mean it could be Dr Vulpus.
Nadia Something might have happened to him.
Madge Anyone coming with me?

Pause

No one? There's nothing to be scared of, you know. Is there?
Charley It's full of spiders out there. And I thought I heard something scurrying.
Madge Oh. I don't do rats. Have you ever seen their tails?
Bella I read somewhere about this bogus doctor. He lures women to this creaky old house and then he ——
Consuela Yes! Thank you for sharing that with us, Bella.

Pause

What's that?
Vera Sounded like a footstep.
Madge (*calling*) We're all down here. Anyone up there?
Bella I do hope nobody answers.
Consuela Shh!
Bella What?
Nadia Shh!

Charley's mobile phone rings. They all jump. Charley answers the phone

Charley (*into the phone; whispering*) Hallo? ... What? ... Why am I whispering? I don't know. (*She stops whispering*) ... Oh no, darling! Where? ... I suppose I can but ... Oh, all right. Give us ten minutes. OK, I know the place. (*She rings off*) Sorry. Adrian — my husband — he's broken down on the bypass. I've got to collect him.
Nadia Oh no ...
Bella Must you?
Charley I'll be back. I might be back. Don't hold your breath though. Sorry. You will tell me what happens?
Consuela Can't your husband wait?
Charley Men don't do waiting. They're like children. See you.

Charley hurries out

Bella shivers

Ghost Night

Vera It's getting so cold in here. I shall complain if no-one else does.
Bella All that was just an excuse for Charley to get away. You know what a scaredy-cat she is.

A distant clock strikes nine during the following; an echoing chime quiet enough for the characters to speak over

Madge Nine o'clock already!
Bella I don't think this Dr Doodah is coming.
Nadia Oh, let's go. We can just catch the Happy Hour at the *Salisbury Arms*.
Madge We can't leave. He's been paid. And cashed the cheque no doubt.
Consuela If you want a job done badly, pay in advance.
Madge If anyone'd like the booking job they're welcome.

Pause

Thought not.
Nadia Talking of paying, I've *got* to spend a penny. I can't wait any longer.
Vera There must be a bathroom upstairs.
Consuela The upstairs lights are not working. I tried.
Vera You'll have to feel your way up the banisters.
Nadia Oh, yes, indeed! I'm not going up there in the dark. Supposing I met something on the stairs!
Bella That's right. There's this film I saw. There's this woman feeling her way upstairs in the dark and she puts her hand on someone's dead face ...
Consuela I wish you wouldn't go on like that!
Vera If it was dark how did she know it was someone's dead face?
Bella She put her fingers up his nostrils.
Consuela (*very edgily*) *Thank* you!
Nadia I can go down that pub. It's only in the next road.
Vera Use the garden. I always do.
Madge This isn't Basildon, Vera!
Bella You'll have to buy a drink in the pub. The *Ferret and Firkin* don't welcome toilet hoppers.

Nadia You couldn't come with us, could you, Vera?
Vera Oh, all right. I could do with a brandy — it's the cold.
Madge Please don't go. You can't leave us on our own!
Vera We won't be a minute.
Madge Well, hurry up back. There'll only be four of us left.
Bella Five. With the ghost.
Consuela Must you?
Bella Thought you didn't *believe* in ghosts?
Nadia We'll be back. Honest.

Nadia and Vera leave

Madge Mind that step ...
Consuela They're not coming back, you know. They're never coming back.

There is a pause. Wendy bursts into tears, sobbing

Bella It's all right, Wend. Don't cry. Just 'cos they're not coming back.
Wendy It's not that. All right ... (*She opens her case, revealing her clothes etc.*) That's all I could pack in the time. He slung me out.
Bella Malcolm? Why, love?
Wendy He caught me with this bloke and well, we didn't have much on ...
Bella (*eagerly*) I think you'd better tell us about it.
Consuela I thought there was something going on!
Wendy I didn't do anything. That's why it's so unfair.
Madge What happened then?
Wendy I was having a bath and I heard Samantha fighting — that's my cat and she always loses and that's another vets' bill — so I grabbed a towel and ran down to the front door to let her in — as you do — and of course I couldn't find her so I went out to call her — and the front door banged shut behind me ...
Bella Well, go on. Go on.
Wendy But that wasn't a problem. I've got a spare key next door with Sarah; so I wrap the towel round me and I run round there and bang on her door. Of course she's not in, is she? Tuesday's her

Aikido night. But her boyfriend's there. Chris. And he's taking a bath and all and he opens the door just with a towel on. It seems so funny and we have a real laugh. So I collect the key and he says he'll come round and help 'cos the spare key's difficult to turn. And you're not going to believe this ...
Bella Try us, love.
Wendy Well, he lets me in and this is the funny thing. *His* door bangs shut so *he* has to come round *my* flat and come in.
Consuela Oh dear.
Wendy I know what you're all thinking but we're having a good laugh about it, a real giggle and then — guess what? Malcolm walks in. Well, he takes one look at us in our towels, puts two and two together to make seven and turns on his heel. He shouts over his shoulder, "I'll be back in one hour. Don't be here. Either of you." And I thought if he doesn't trust me I may as well *not* be here. I'll collect my cat tomorrow. Anyway, it's all over with Malcolm now.
Bella That is just typical man. It's men they don't trust and they're right not to.
Consuela Where are you going to go?
Wendy I don't know, do I?
Madge It's all right, love. You can stay with us. But I'll have to talk to my feller, Danny. He's only down Save-it-All on the check-out. I can't call him 'cos they don't allow that but I can buy a packet of fags and then I can chat to him. It'll be all right. I'll phone you on this number. (*She picks up the phone*) It's working. I'm fed up waiting for this Dr Tiddleypush anyway.
Consuela Don't go, Madge! We'll be down to three if you do!
Madge I've got to go on home and get a room ready for Wendy. (*To Wendy*) You are coming, aren't you?
Wendy Oh, Madge, could I?
Madge Right. Have fun, you lot. Ta-ra.
Wendy Oh ta, Madge.

Madge exits

Bella And then there were three.
Consuela Well, we're not leaving, are we?

Suddenly the radio starts playing music, making Bella, Wendy and Consuela jump

Bella Who turned that on?
Wendy I never touched it.
Consuela Nor did I — but somebody did ...
Bella I'll switch it off.
Consuela No! Don't go near it! It might ...
Bella Might what?
Consuela I don't know.

Bella switches the radio off

I don't know what we're doing here at all.
Bella I think you're right, love. I don't know what we're doing here. We've got nothing to prove, have we? And ... Oh my God, I forgot! I've got to go and check my kitchen. I'm sure I left the gas on!
Consuela Let's all go and check your kitchen.
Wendy I can't. I've got to wait for Madge.
Consuela That's all right then. You wait for Madge and I'll go with Bella.
Bella We can't leave her alone. It's like those films where the girl goes into the old house and everyone shouts "Don't go down the cellar on your own!" — but she does.
Consuela Come with us, Wendy.
Wendy I've got nowhere to go ... Don't leave me all on my own. I've got to wait for the phone call. I'm afraid of being on my own in my own flat — but here ...
Bella Oh, all right. We'll stay. Just for a few minutes more.
Consuela Er ... You see — I've got the church flowers to do. For tomorrow.
Bella I've never seen you like this before, love — all edgy and uptight.
Consuela I'm not edgy. I'm not! Heavens! I've just remembered. I've got to check the dates on my library books!

Ghost Night

Bella What?
Consuela Charles hates paying fines. And I get the blame.
Bella I've heard it all now! Library books! Well, you go. I'll look after Wendy. I'm not afraid of ghosts. As long as they don't turn up.

The sound of a fire engine is heard

Wendy That sounds like an ambulance! I hope Malcolm hasn't done anything daft!
Bella No! That's a fire engine! I *knew* I'd left the gas on!
Consuela Oh, don't be silly. It could be anyone's house — some child with his head stuck in the railings ...
Bella It's my house! I know it! I've got to get there quick. I'm sorry!
Consuela You can't go!
Bella It's an emergency! Sorry ... (*She heads for the exit*)
Consuela (*calling out, in a panic*) There's only two of us left!

Bella exits

There is a silence

I felt it, you know. As soon as I came into the house.
Wendy Felt it?
Consuela The atmosphere. There's something evil here. Evil, I tell you. Something monstrous. It's affected us all ...
Wendy I thought you didn't believe in all that!
Consuela I ... I pretend not to. To keep it away. To keep my life nice and tidy. Nothing wrong with that, is there? But it's got rid of all the others, hasn't it? And it's coming for me! Thank God you're here, Wendy!
Wendy But I ... I've always been afraid of everything ...
Consuela No. That's me. All blether and bombast. But underneath, just quaking! Prayers. Do you know any prayers? I mean I go to church every Sunday but ... "Dearly beloved" ... No, that's the marriage service. Bell, book and candle ... We haven't got a bell or a book — or a candle.

Wendy (*not listening*) It's a funny thing. I was terrified of Malcolm walking out and me being alone but when he did — I wasn't afraid of being alone any more.

Consuela It's me who's alone. My husband left me years ago. He's still there of course but he's left me all right.

The Lights go out suddenly leaving just the dim glow from the hall

Oh no! Not the dark! (*She grabs Wendy*)

Wendy Someone's grabbed hold of me!

Consuela It's me. Don't leave me, Wendy!

Wendy You're strangling me ... Who's turned out the lights?

Consuela It's them. They did all this. Waiting for me. They have no need for light. Don't you see? They don't need the light!

Wendy Do you think — someone could be trying to frighten us?

Consuela They're doing a wonderful job. (*She starts to cry*) I can't stand it, Wendy, I can't ... (*She knocks the phone over*) Oh, the phone! It must have moved! It wasn't there before! Who moved it then? There's only the two of us here!

Wendy Cold blast of air. Feel it? That must mean it's here.

Consuela Oh, my God ... Hold on — I think I know what to do.

Wendy What? Well, try it. Anything ... Where are you?

Consuela Just here. Just here by the door. It's all right.

Wendy I think I know a prayer — hymn — (*Singing*) "He who would valiant be, let him come hither ..."

Consuela You'd be better off without me. Honestly you would.

Wendy Consuela! Don't go! Don't leave me with — with it.

Consuela exits

(*Singing*) "She who would be valiant be — 'gainst all disaster ..."

The Lights come on

Oh, thank God! (*Looking about her*) Consuela? Consuela? (*She jumps up*) Is that you out there? Don't play games, Consuela.

The front door slams

I knew it. I knew it! This is my nightmare! I'll wake up in a minute. (*She closes her eyes, then opens them*) I'm still here. It isn't a dream. Alone. Why do I always get left alone? And it's coming for me. I can hear it! (*She puts her hands over her face in despair and sobs briefly. She takes her hands away*) I must cut my nails ... What? Huh! (*She realizes she's not really afraid*) Well, well! That's just how you'd *expect* me to behave. All right, Malcolm ... All right, ladies ... (*Suddenly shouting*) All right then, come and get me! (*She walks up to the table and snatches off the tablecloth*) Nothing! (*She goes to the covered chair and snatches off the sheet, revealing the two cushions*) Nothing! Nothing but shadows. *My* shadows!

The front door is heard to open

Ah. So there is something. Here you come then. And I'm ready for you! (*She grabs the large jug*)

The Lights go off again

Oh yes, you're in charge of all the effects, aren't you? I don't care. I'm damned if I'm going to be frightened.

We hear cautious footsteps

Malcolm, a tall dark figure of indefinite silhouette (indefinite because he is carrying a very large bunch of flowers) enters and stands by the door

Wendy screams and holds the jug up high, preparing to smash the newcomer on the head

The Lights come on

Malcolm Wendy!

Wendy Malcolm?
Malcolm Why did you scream?
Wendy I ... I was trying to frighten you.
Malcolm You did.
Wendy What are you doing here?
Malcolm Bella told me you were here. Put that bloody thing down. I came to say sorry. Chris next door told me what happened with the cat and the bath towel ... I just jumped to the wrong conclusion. I'm very sorry.
Wendy I'm spending the night in a haunted house, thanks to you!
Malcolm Haunted house? No, it's not. Madge called. She tried to phone you but you were engaged. You've all been in the wrong house. This is 7, Hangingtree Hill. Dr Vulpus is down at 7, Harrington Hill, waiting for his audience. Now that *is* a haunted house!
Wendy So what's this place then?
Malcolm I don't know. It's somebody's ... So let's get out of here.
Wendy Yes, but strange things happened — the TV, the radio, the lights ...
Malcolm (*checking the electrics just outside the door*) Oh, I see. There's a time switch. Anti-burglar thing. Shall we go home, darling?
Wendy I don't know if I want to. Haven't made up my mind yet.
Malcolm Have to. Your cat's up a sixty-foot tree next door. Sarah called the fire brigade. We can't stay here.
Wendy I could. I could stay anywhere. I'm not afraid. And I'm not afraid of you either. Oh, all right. Pick up that case.
Malcolm Yes, dear. (*He picks up Wendy's case*)
Wendy Walk.
Malcolm Right.

Malcolm exits with the case

Wendy follows Malcolm and pauses in the doorway

Wendy Good-night, dear ghosts. Go to sleep. (*She heads off*) Oh. And thanks for everything.

Wendy exits, closing the door

There is a moment's silence

The table lamp moves. It slowly slides off the table and crashes to the floor. The gramophone plays

CURTAIN

FURNITURE AND PROPERTY LIST

On stage: Small table. *On it*: cloth, old-fashioned lamp, Bakelite dial telephone, large china jug
Chair. *On it*: two cushions and none-too-clean sheet
Tribal mask
Stuffed animal
Old television
Old-fashioned mains radio
Wind-up gramophone
Pile of 78 rpm records

Off stage: Torch and bag containing programme of events, thermos flask, packets of biscuits (**Madge**)
Umbrella (**Consuela**)
Stick (**Vera**)
Suitcase containing clothes and other belongings (**Wendy**)

Personal: **Charley**: mobile phone

LIGHTING PLOT

To open: Darkness; dim glow on hallway backing

Cue 1	**Madge** switches the lights on *Bring up general interior lighting*	(Page 1)
Cue 2	**Madge**: "You wanted to come, love." *Bring up TV flicker effect*	(Page 3)
Cue 3	**Consuela**:" It's probably indigestion." *Fade TV lighting effect*	(Page 3)
Cue 4	**Consuela**: " ... but he's left me all right." *Cut general interior lighting*	(Page 16)
Cue 5	**Wendy**: "—'gainst all disaster." *Restore general interior lighting*	(Page 16)
Cue 6	**Wendy** grabs the large jug *Cut general interior lighting*	(Page 17)
Cue 7	**Wendy** screams and holds the jug up high *Restore general interior lighting*	(Page 17)

EFFECTS PLOT

Cue 1	As play begins *Music from gramophone;* *runs down after a few seconds*	(Page 1)
Cue 2	**Madge**: " … a hundred and eighty-six." *Phone rings*	(Page 6)
Cue 3	**Nadia**: "Shh!" **Charley**'s *mobile phone rings*	(Page 10)
Cue 4	**Bella**: " ... what a scaredy-cat she is." *Clock strikes nine*	(Page 11)
Cue 5	**Consuela**: "Well, we're not leaving, are we?" *Radio starts playing music*	(Page 13)
Cue 6	**Bella** switches the radio off *Cut music*	(Page 14)
Cue 7	**Bella**: "As long as they don't turn up." *Fire engine sound*	(Page 15)
Cue 8	**Wendy** exits. A moment's silence *Table lamp moves and crashes to the floor.* *Music from gramophone*	(Page 19)

A licence issued by Samuel French Ltd to perform this play does not include permission to use the Incidental music specified in this copy. Where the place of performance is already licensed by the PERFORMING RIGHT SOCIETY a return of the music used must be made to them. If the place of performance is not so licensed then application should be made to the Performing Right Society, 29 Berners Street, London W1.

A separate and additional licence from PHONOGRAPHIC PERFORMANCES LTD, 1 Upper James Street, London W1R 3HG is needed whenever commercial recordings are used.